Y0-BZD-272

TRACES

An Investigation in Reason

John A. Chakeres

Nuance Press Inc. • *1977*

Copyright © 1977 by John A. Chakeres

All rights reserved. No portion of this book may be reproduced in any form by anyone, without written permission of the photographer or publisher.

Library of Congress Card Number: 76-47816
International Standard Book Number: 0-917924-00-2

Exclusive Distributor: Light Impressions Corporation
Post Office Box 3012 • Rochester, New York 14614

Published by: Nuance Press Inc.
542 North High Street • Columbus, Ohio 43215

First Printing 1977 • Manufactured in the United States of America

TRACES

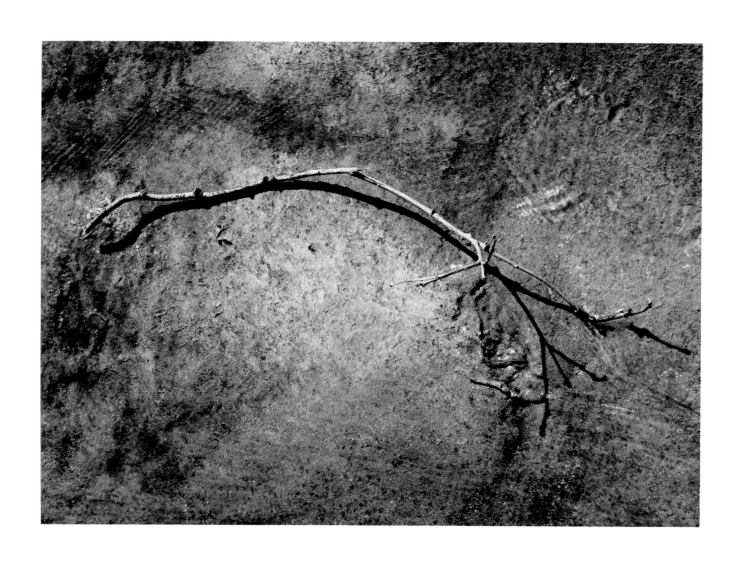

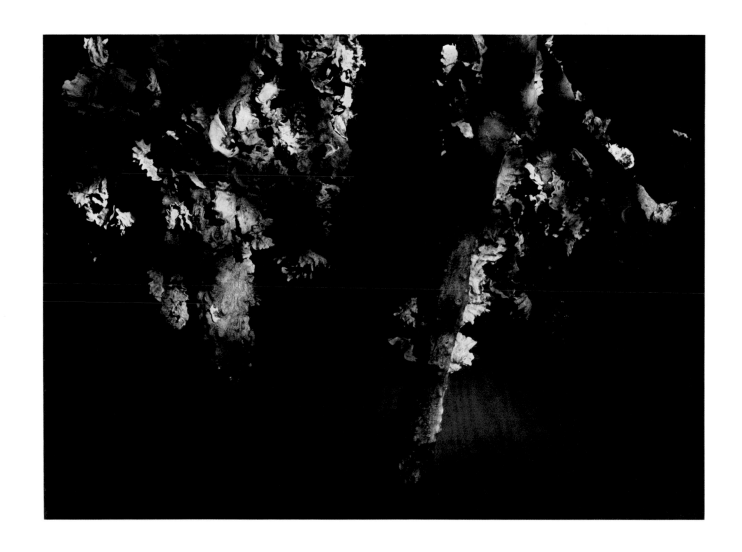

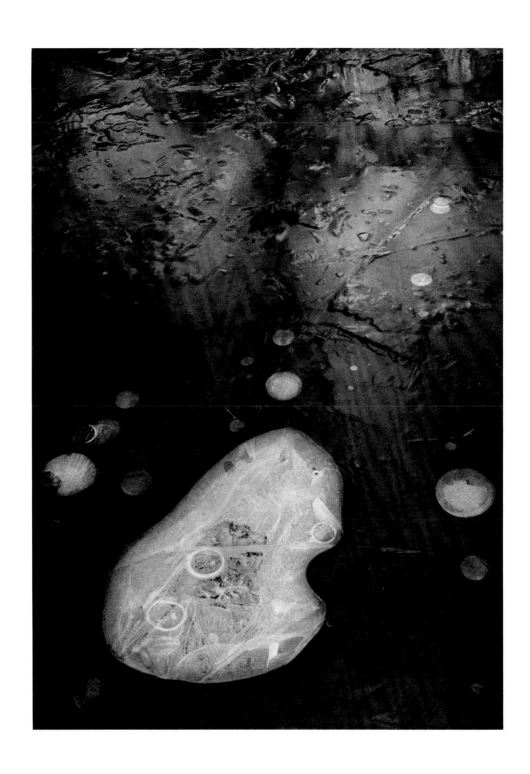

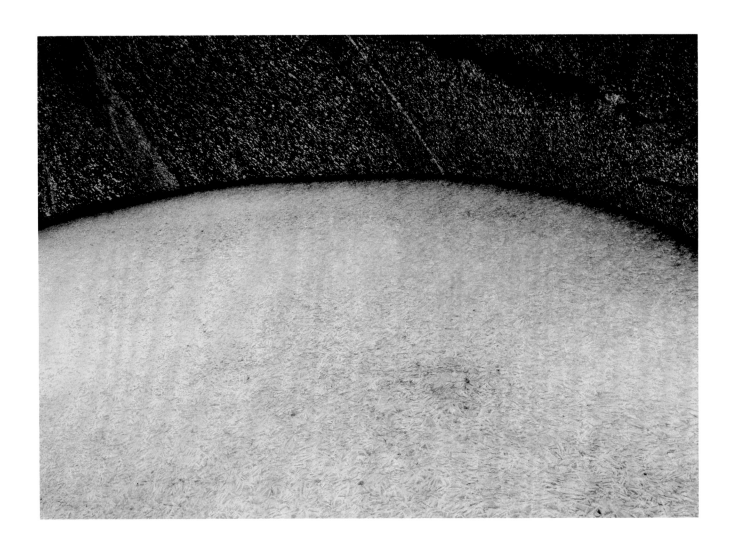

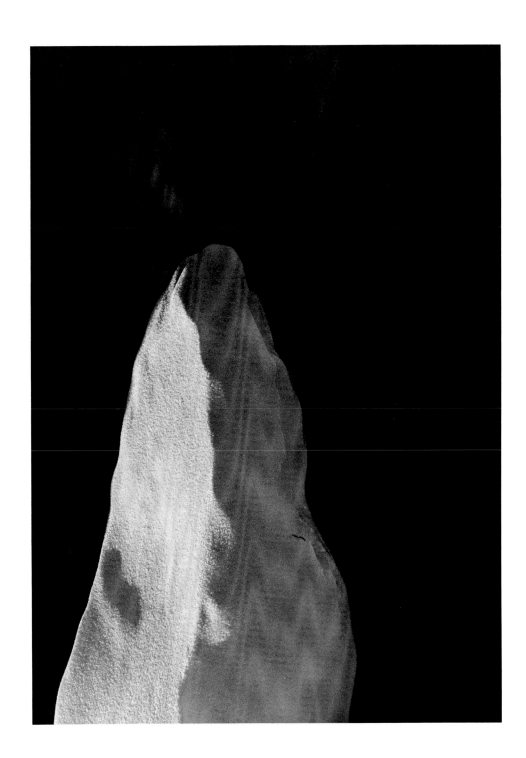

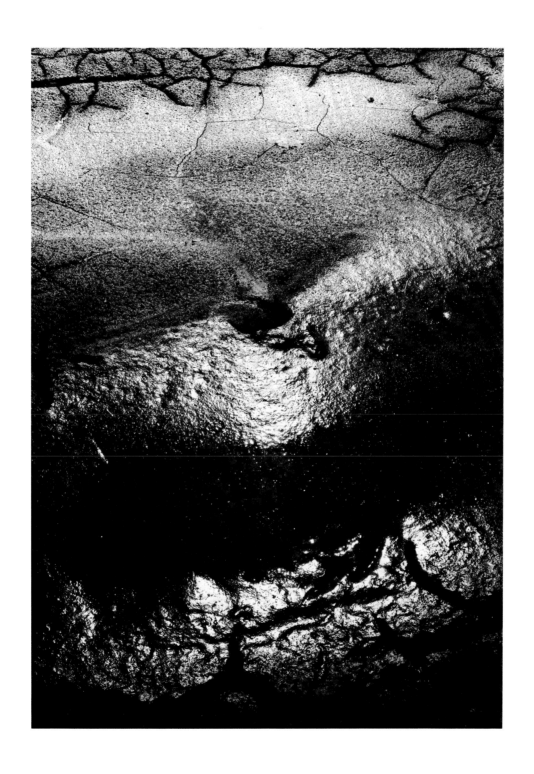

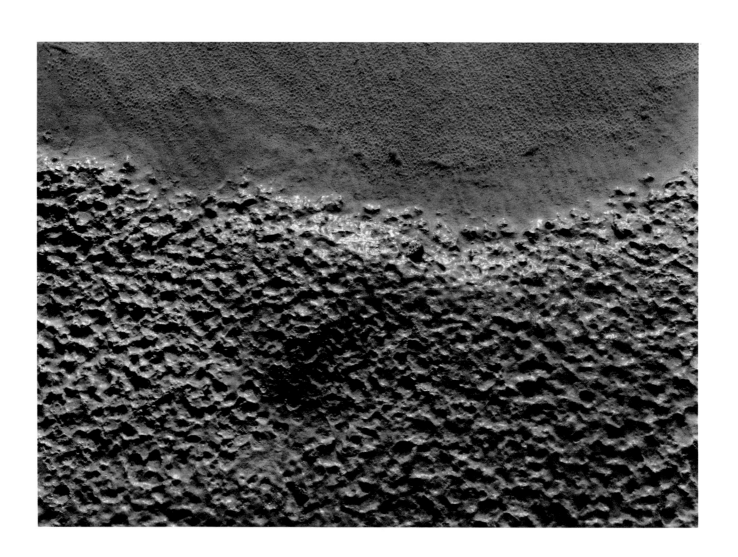

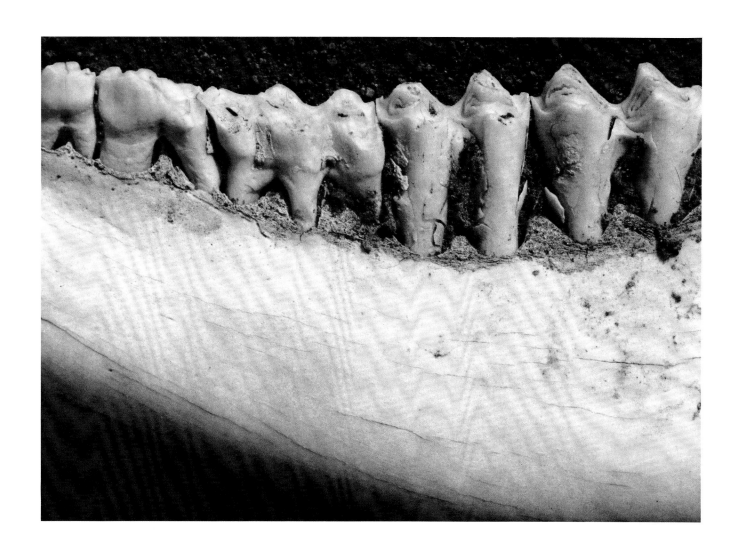

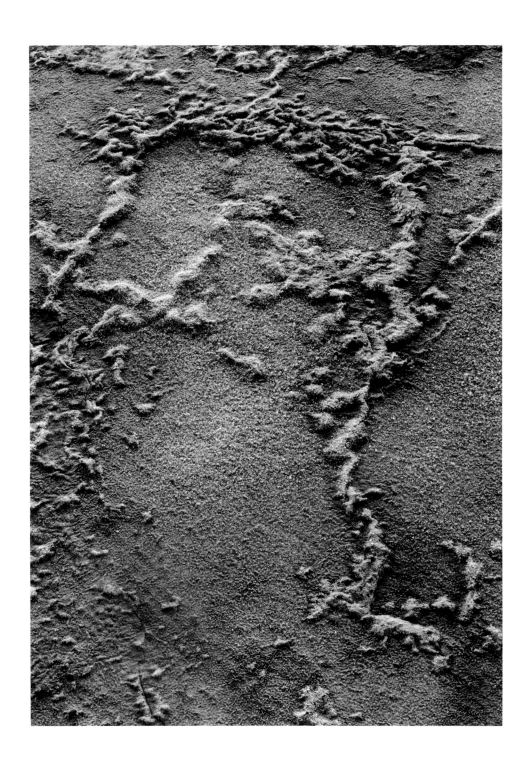

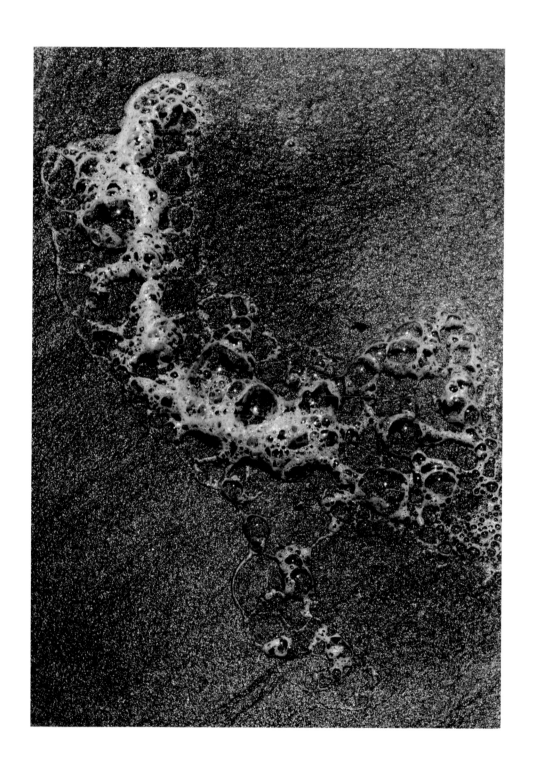

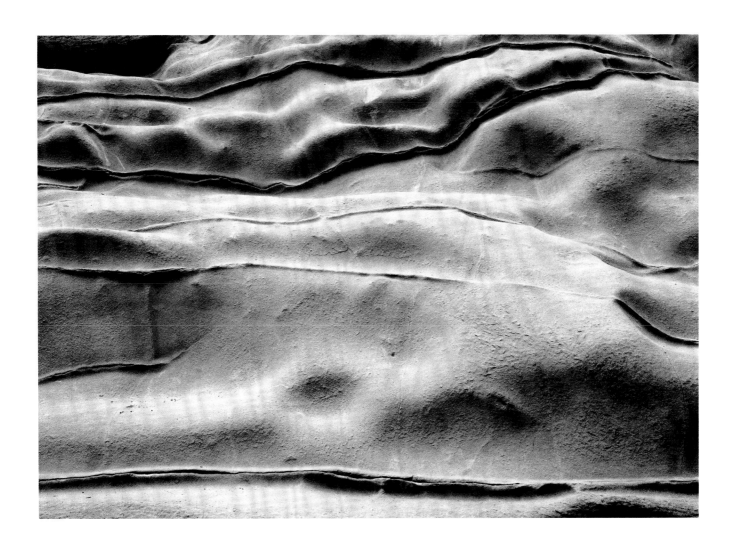

Afterword

During the course of our lives a semblance of the past can be seen within the various objects we collect. Many of them are discarded but a few are retained for a variety of reasons, each having some significance for the individual. If the remaining objects are grouped in some form an interesting change takes place; they begin to lose their singular qualities and merge with the others to form an abstract image of the past. This new information can now be used as a means to gain knowledge and insight about ourselves. We can also look back upon our lives and see who we were and perhaps a hint as to what we might become. And if enough time is spent with the knowledge it will ultimately reveal a meaning to the enigma we call life.

Understanding and purpose are all we really seek in life and all that will remain of the pursuit are a few Traces.

Colophon

Traces was designed by John Chakeres and Al Mazzarella. The printing was by Carl Sesto of Pentacle Press in two impression offset lithography; Mark Orlove, camera-man. The text paper is Warren's 100 pound Cameo dull; the endpapers are Strathmore Artlaid and the cover, Strathmore Pastelle. The type, Dante, was set by Michael and Winifred Bixler, with Katy Homans. The books were bound by Robert Burlen and Son.

I would like to thank the following for all their help on this project: Mr. & Mrs. James W. Chakeres, my parents; Carl Sesto, Steve Crouch, Al Mazzarella, Kathe Keller, Katy Homans, and Slick, my cat.

Traces was completed in January, 1977.

J. A. C.